BULLETIN BOARDS AND DISPLAY

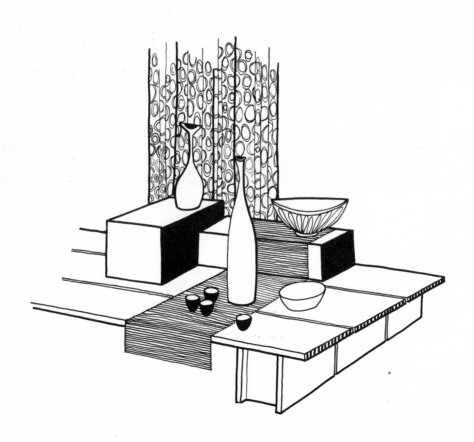

BULLETIN BOARDS AND DISPLAY

REINO RANDALL Associate Professor of Art, Central Washington State College, Ellensburg, Washington
EDWARD C. HAINES Associate Professor of Art, Central Washington State College, Ellensburg, Washington
DARWIN DAVIS — Drawings

DAVIS PUBLICATIONS, INC. • PRINTERS BUILDING • WORCESTER, MASSACHUSETTS

● ACKNOWLEDGMENTS

To our former students who have demonstrated the value of display in their own teaching experience; to our colleagues and friends who have been generous in advice and encouragement; and the individuals and institutions whose photographs are reproduced with permission, we express our thanks.   THE AUTHORS

CONTENTS

FOREWORD

In preparing this manual we have attempted to state simple, time-tested principles and suggestions which, upon study, will help you create effective educational displays. We have placed the stress on functional and esthetic values, recognizing that the purpose of the classroom display is the distribution of information while satisfying high artistic standards.

While numerous illustrations show our solutions, we encourage you and your students to create unique and personal displays tailored to your classroom situations. There is no one formula for good design. Any creative, inspirational approach to the many areas of study which can be illustrated by imaginative displays will increase design skills in both teacher and students. Awareness of display opportunities in the classroom will develop with the practice of the principles suggested here.

RWR
ECH

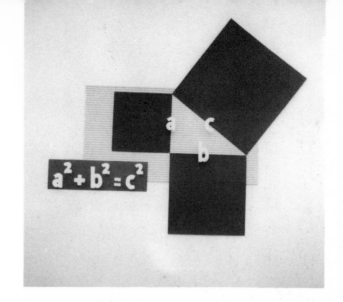

Aware of the need for communication, teachers and professional display artists observe the same principles in their presentation. Good design speaks clearly.

MAURICE GROSSMAN (PHOTO)

7

HOW DISPLAY WORKS FOR YOU

THE DISPLAY AS AN EDUCATIONAL TOOL

Classroom display may cover a broad range from a simple bulletin board to a larger comprehensive display, including three-dimensional groupings. A display which is properly planned and controlled can be artistically valuable as well as educational:

- children can visualize abstract concepts which are difficult to grasp verbally.
- opportunities may be provided for direct sensory experience in three-dimensional exhibits.
- color and form help to arouse interest.
- cooperation and committee work are helpful in the development of leadership and self-confidence.
- the learning environment can be made more colorful and exciting with graphic displays.

In presenting up-to-the-minute information, the display often transcends the textbook and focuses attention directly on the changing issues of the day. Gathered around a timely bulletin board an entire class may be taught from a presentation of events, names and places in the news. Such topics take on new significance when brought to the attention of the class as a gigantic textbook. Motivation, retention and learning result from a graphic presentation.

The sources of educational display materials are as rich and varied as our omnipresent newspapers, today's colorful magazines, posters, maps and models which are available everywhere. Art material companies, museums, libraries and large businesses often circulate informative exhibitions at small cost to schools. The addition of student collections of reproductions and clippings to the variety of materials gathered by the teacher will insure a perpetual supply of resource items that can be within the reach of all.

The most impelling displays are those which are carefully integrated with other learning, and frequently reviewed. With guidance and suggestion from the teacher, this visual method of teaching can be student-motivated and student-organized with committees selecting the themes and performing the necessary mechanics of arrangement. Such committees may function for a single occasion, a unit of study or longer. With teacher instruction and class evaluation, the entire process can be learned by individuals and groups. For suggestions on the capability levels of the various age groups, see the chart on page 60.

THE DISPLAY AS A CREATIVE EXPERIENCE

As a creative experience the display offers a practical art problem in which idea, selection of appropriate materials, execution and evaluation afford certain opportunities not present in desk and easel work. This is especially helpful in developing, in those students whose art contacts have been limited, good taste in design and color, and a new awareness of the beauty to be found all around them.

Large scale manipulation of color, line, texture, form and space is directly related to such areas of art production as mural, stage and advertising design, as well as window display. A teen-age student whose work is cramped or whose subject matter is stereotyped may be forced, by the nature of the display materials, to create design solutions of greater freedom of scope and area. If an entire class is engaged in a project, group discussion and criticism will help each individual in the development of lasting art values. An effective design, and the discovery of those elements which contribute to it may, for example, lead to a surer knowledge of such vital tools of design as color, lettering, and the use of space. Once the habit of analysis is established, it can be extended to other areas of the visual world: newspapers, magazines, store advertisements and the fine arts.

Considered in the light of its educational and esthetic implications, the school display, while no panacea for all educational problems, is an indispensable and exciting educational tool.

Prompt removal of the display when it has served its purpose is important because, if allowed to remain, it can become stale and meaningless. If the display materials are sorted and filed they will be readily available for future use. A file of thumbnail sketches of effective exhibits already used can serve as a helpful reference.

THE DISPLAY AS A PUBLICITY DEVICE

Parents, visitors to the school, and administrators quickly catch the spirit of the school and its activities when colorful and impelling presentations vitalize corridors and classrooms. Favorable relations with the public can be achieved through displays which are judiciously placed in libraries, store windows and other prominent locations. Thus, the dynamic qualities of art are demonstrated by these practical and tangible displays.

DISPLAY IN THE LIBRARY

Display and books are a natural combination, mutually complementing and reinforcing their common purposes. Each represents a means of dispersing knowledge and exciting interest, the former through the word symbol, and the latter through the visual symbol. Librarians recognize the varied contributions of the display to their work :

- to stimulate an interest in reading for education and pleasure.
- to inform and describe library procedures.
- to publicize and acquaint the reading public with new acquisitions.
- to assist teachers with special units of study.
- to provide a colorful and interesting atmosphere.
- to celebrate and emphasize special days.

Materials for the Library Display

- book jackets which should be retained and filed.
- children's collections of insects, toys, etc.
- borrowed collections (pioneer artifacts, etc.)
- local museum material
- paper sculpture (one of the most useful and accessible display items)
- puppets
- clippings, maps, reproductions
- books

Suggestions for Library Display

- place one or two books or pamphlets on a sheet of colored paper with appropriate objects. Observe heights carefully.
- display books with flowers or dried arrangements.
- combine the bulletin board with small shelves or a table on which are placed a few books; relate books and board with streamers or yarn.
- create a mobile type of book display with book jackets.
- use the window sills for display.
- use one shelf of a prominent book case for three-dimensional display.
- combine portraits of book characters or prominent men and biographies.

The curve of the symbolic olive branch counteracts the vertical movement established by the rectangular format and lettering in this effective layout. In a complicated arrangement, unlike two- and three-dimensional forms are harmonized by a controlling background organization.

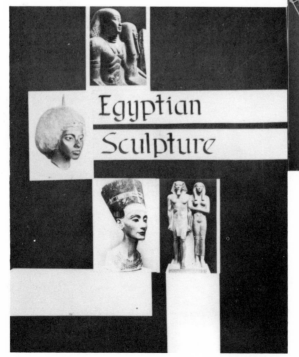

Three distinctive bulletin boards, each characterized by a geometric layout. Stro[ng] contrasts of dark and light insure visibili[ty] across the room. Negative areas are carefully designed.

PRINCIPLES TO GUIDE YOU

Displays are organized according to certain principles which are common to the expressional arts and serve the same useful purpose. We can judge the artistic merit of our work and insure a degree of psychological effectiveness by observing these simple guides:

SIMPLICITY

Simplify shapes, lines, spaces and colors in order to present a readable display. A good rule to follow: "When in doubt, leave it out!"

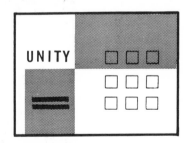

a. Restrict your display to a few carefully selected colors.

b. Do not crowd too much material into one space. It is better to plan a series of displays with a great quantity of material.

c. Avoid being arty or pretty, which involves decoration without reason. Present your material with emphasis on organization, color, and texture, and not on "cuteness."

d. To secure attention and carry your message, surround your displayed material with empty space.

e. Avoid distracting, patchy subject headings. Relate labels.

f. Place informational captions in limited areas or units inside the display area, not at the edges.

UNITY

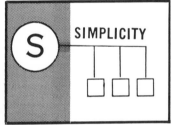

a. A dominance of similar shapes, lines and space will help to maintain a family relationship. Disunity is distracting.

b. Emphasize a basic line direction throughout the design. You will observe that the block organization is used extensively in the illustrations.

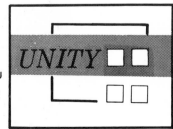

EMPHASIS

a. To focus attention on any important item, set it apart with isolating space, value contrast, color contrast, texture contrast.

b. Point out or encircle an important area with a directional device such as an arrow, line or string.

c. Project the illustration into space with a three-dimensional device like a box on which the material is mounted.

BALANCE

a. Informal balance creates more interest than does formal balance.

b. Formal balance represents an equal distribution of visual weights which invites quick and final inspection and stresses dignity in the design.

c. The diagonal plan should be avoided because it creates two awkward areas on either side of the diagonal axis and urges the eye to move quickly out of the display.

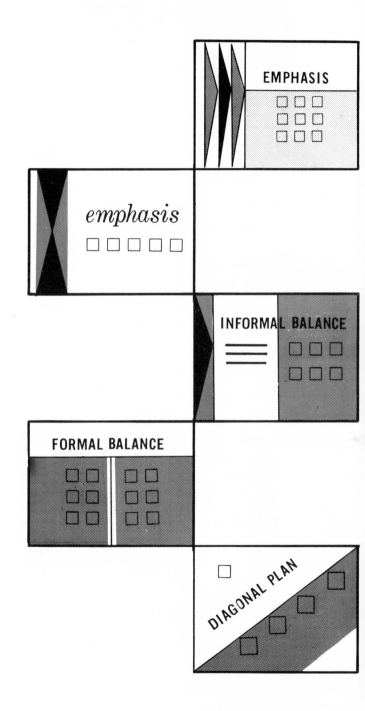

1 An appropriate and simple greeting which should appeal to the primary level. The dark line on the light background unifies the two large areas of the composition.

2 The parts of this informal layout are unified by a string line against a background of textural material.

3 Texture, value, and line are used symbolically to create a dramatic display.

4 An informal balance of units is directed into the display rather than out. Torn paper shapes are in harmony with the character of the subject.

Observe the non-rectangular plan, the directional devices which lead the eye through the design, the maximum contrast of values which carry across the room, and the vertical organization of the five units which constitute a block.

VISUAL TOOLS

For the purposes of clarity we have isolated and identified the various visual components of the display, but these elements are not separated in practice. All parts work together to convey a total unity. The successful arrangement is the integrated sum of the parts designed to present an attractive and clear-speaking display.

LINE

Line has several functions; it is a structural device, and an eyecatcher.

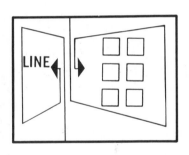

a. It can attract attention by pulling the eye to a specific area. Yarn or string lead to important parts.

b. It can suggest action, direction, and movement. Lines suggest that we go along.

c. It can hold the display together; it can tie all parts within a border.

SHAPE

A shape or form may be two-dimensional (a flat form like paper) or three-dimensional (like paper sculpture projecting into space and having a light and dark shadow pattern).

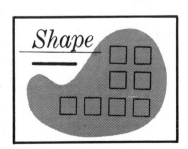

a. A cut paper shape may serve as a background for illustration and lettering.

b. Repeating a similar mount or mat brings "like-ness" and creates harmony. Beware of too many strange shapes.

c. Actual objects fastened to the background arouse interest. Examples: weeds, shells, milk carton, etc.

COLOR

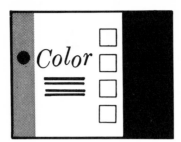

Color, the most sensuous of the elements, commands attention, helps to clarify, and brings pleasure.

  a. No color works alone; color changes in the neighborhood of another color.

  b. Color is traditionally symbolic (yellow-green for spring, red for valentines), but we should dare to invent new color symbols for traditional symbols.

  c. Unusual color friendships or combinations attract attention (orange and pink).

  d. Intense color assumes visual impact (bright orange against black.)

  e. Light and dark color values carry to every seat in the room.

  f. Patterns of color lead the eye from area to area giving the sensation of movement.

TEXTURE, or the feel of things, invites visual or touch inspection.

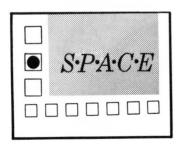

  a. Visual shock by contrast of surfaces attracts attention (foil opposed to sandpaper).

  b. Texture holds our interest because the feel of things gives us pleasure.

  c. Texture makes an environment for our display by providing background (burlap or corrugated cardboard).

SPACE

The display utilizing depth (the third dimension) provides an environment with which we are familiar since we exist in a spatial world

  a. Background areas must receive careful attention and must, in themselves, constitute good shapes.

  b. All material shows to best advantage if surrounded by ample empty space. Loosely arranged material scattered in a sea of space creates lonely islands, but objects overlapped or moved together create visual units.

  c. Space is created by advancing and receding colors and by lights and darks.

  d. To vitalize a display, project objects into space. Example: a sea shell, letters casting shadows.

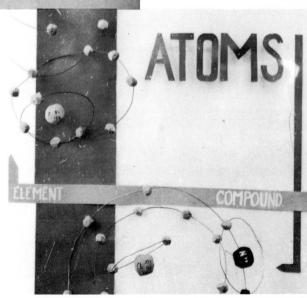

Rich and varied illustrative materials are played against a simple background which provides the stability required for active illustrations. Shapes, colors and captions, without graphic illustrations, often perform effectively.

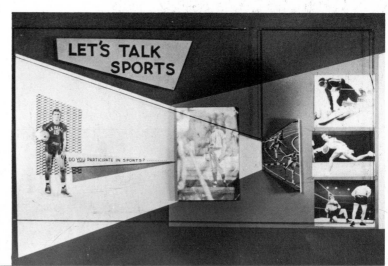

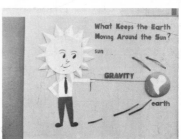

Lettering is always an integral part of the total design and will fulfill its purpose if it is related in scale and in character to the spirit of the display. An appropriate alphabet, good value contrast, and accurate spacing are necessary to a well planned display.

PLANNING THE DISPLAY

The school display will make its need felt. A season, a discussion, an event or some current school situation will suggest a bulletin board. Or when pertinent, illustrative materials are available, a display will result. Once teachers and students become aware of the value of graphic demonstration they will progress in techniques and the many purposes of display.

Because so much material is available today, the temptation is to use too much. This weakens the impact of the message. The effective arrangement is the economical one which is dominated by a single idea, or a group of closely related ideas receiving varying degrees of emphasis.

1. DECIDE ON WHAT TO DISPLAY   Current events, newspaper clippings, photographs, maps, people and places.
   Hobbies — stamps, shells, insect collections.
   Class work — social studies, arithmetic, writing, spelling.
   Art work — drawings, paintings, sculpture, crafts.

2. CHOOSE A CATCHY CAPTION   Students are quick to distill the spirit of the display and to choose a caption which will attract the passer-by. Imaginative use of words, shock value, a question which demands an answer are devices to excite attention. It should be brief, colorful, to-the-point and in harmony with the display. Current advertising situations slogans or humorous television titles can often be paraphrased.

3. SKETCH A PLAN   Several quick sketches of the layout including background material, illustrations and lettering will save time.

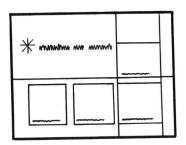 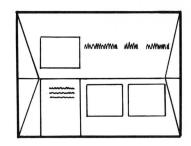 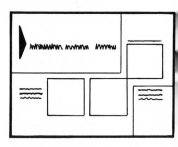

4. PREARRANGE THE MATERIAL   On the work table, a trial layout following the sketched plan gives opportunity for evaluation and change in the arrangement as necessary

5. SET UP THE DISPLAY   Install the display with the best fastening device: pins, stapler, thumb tacks, map pins, masking tape with one or two glued surfaces.

6. EVALUATE THE DISPLAY   In judging your work, and in the class discussion which is an integral part of the procedure, the following questions should be considered:

- Does it attract attention? How?
- Have we applied the principles of simplicity, unity, balance and emphasis?
- Is the message clear and communicative?
- Do the illustrations, lettering and background harmonize?
- Does it pass the test of good taste and attractiveness?
- How can it be improved?

USING THE DISPLAY

The school display is an essential and effective teaching device, since children are involved
both in its creation and its use. It can be eloquent in its presentation of facts, and simple
and economical in emphasizing selected points. Use display as a powerful medium to communicate.

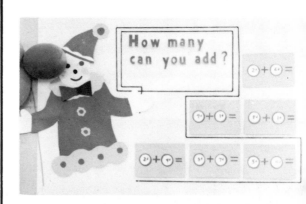

The idea for instructional displays grows directly from school and community needs. To the alert display committee each new situation provides a worthy theme for exposition.

5

MATERIALS OF DISPLAY

What materials shall we use in creating our arrangement once the idea and plan have been determined? To carry out a consistent theme some topics will require specific qualities of texture and color, such as shiny or dull, rough or smooth. Our collection should contain a variety of papers, foils, strings, etc. Regardless of the material chosen, simplicity and good taste must be the underlying factor in the display. Pictorial and realistic effects are inappropriate and teachers who attempt a literal picture with materials overlook the primary purpose of this visual aid. Good criteria can be determined from an analysis of contemporary advertisements and posters.

DISPLAY MATERIALS

BACKGROUND MATERIALS

Burlap
Monk's Cloth
Construction Paper
Corrugated Cardboard

HAND TOOLS

Hammer
Pliers
Screwdriver
Stencil Knife

ART MATERIALS

Opaque water colors
Brush, Pen and Ink

FASTENING ITEMS AND DEVICES

Steel pins on wrist cushion
Upholstery tacks
Brightly colored map pins
Staples and stapler
String and yarn
Wall hooks for hanging

Masking tape, including the
  kind with two adhesive surfaces
Bulletin-board wax
Thumb tacks
Paste and glue
Rubber cement

MISCELLANEOUS MATERIALS

String, wire, thread, yarn
Screen wire, hardware cloth
Cardboard boxes, various sizes
Sponges, beads
Straw mats

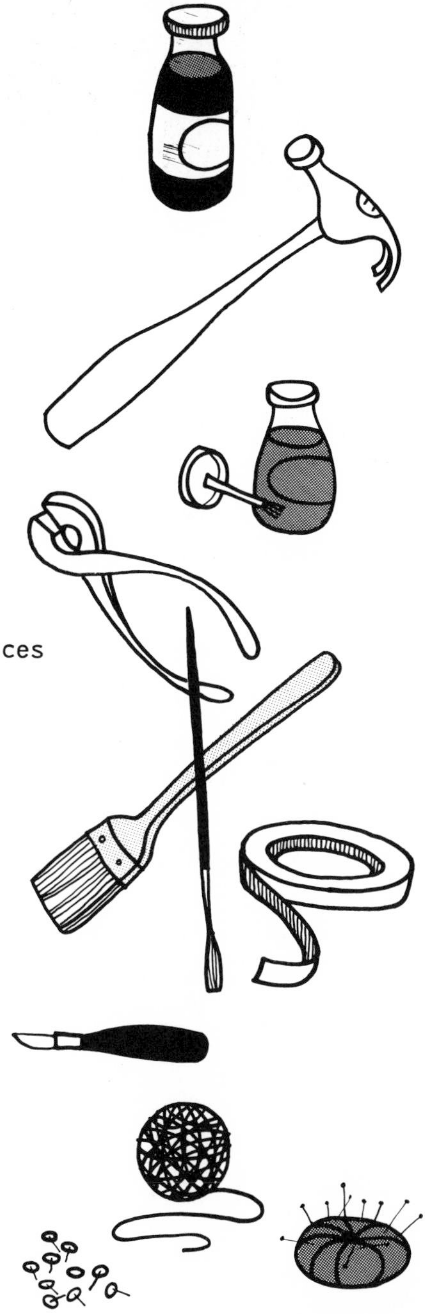

29

THE COMPREHENSIVE EXHIBIT

In the previous chapters of this manual we discussed the two-dimensional or bulletin-board ty
of display which is oriented to the daily classroom activity and adapted primarily to a specifi
classroom audience. In addition, its functional life is short and its scope is limited. We mus
now consider the comprehensive exhibit, the content of which may be art, science or other su
ject. In order to communicate with the public and the school and its administrators, the compr
hensive exhibit is usually planned for special occasions such as a school fair, Parent-Teach
Night, or perhaps as an end-of-the-year summary of accomplishment. An exhibit of this kind is
characterized by the diversity and quantity of material to be shown which create special prob
lems in the use of space. Such is the nature of the large-scale exhibit. The combined efforts
of teachers, students, and committees must be involved in pre-planning its purpose, organiza
tion, and physical mechanics of arrangement.

WHAT IS THE PURPOSE OF THE EXHIBIT?

Is it to explain science in the elementary school or does it illustrate the growth and progress
of art classes during the year? Once the purpose is decided, a controlling theme may be chos
for exposition. All other elements will then fit into a unified plan.

SELECT THE MATERIALS   The best exhibit is planned well in advance of the opening date, from materials available in abundance. From a large resource of drawings, paintings, charts, models, or photographs, a variety of carefully chosen examples should be selected on predetermined criteria such as:

- Is the exhibit content expressive of its purpose?
- Is there a balanced variety, large and small, two- and three-dimensional?
- Is there a fair representation of all students' work?
- If this is to be a sequential or process type of exhibit, are the various steps clearly illustrated and explained?

WHERE IS THE DISPLAY TO BE SHOWN?   Consider the area. A corridor, a classroom, the gymnasium or the cafeteria may provide the large floor space needed.

DRAW A MAP   In order to simplify the placement of all essential elements, the committee should draw up a plan or map to locate, during the pre-planning stage, all those elements which will go into the display. This map might pinpoint the locations of exhibition furniture, doors, windows, captions and lighting facilities. It might also indicate a traffic pattern in and out of the display area.

CONSIDER THE TRAFFIC PATTERN   A wide entrance, well-lighted, colorful with caption or plants, will invite entrance at that point; inside the room all furniture will indicate a natural flow of spectators from entrance to exit.

VISUAL OASIS   Two or three chairs or a bench so placed that viewers can enjoy an attractive area provide a welcome place of rest and conversation.

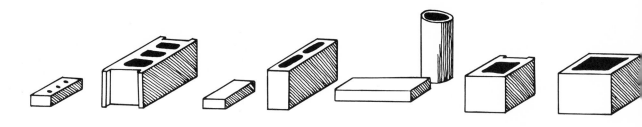

EXHIBITION FURNITURE

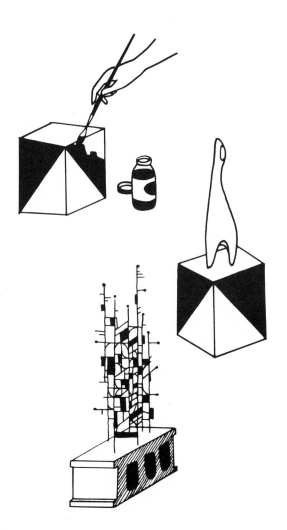

The average school, in the absence of museum equipment, must improvise its exhibition furniture from easels, painted boxes, tables, stools, concrete blocks. Screens which divide the space and add to existing wall space may be constructed of 1" x 2" wood strip frames with soft building board fastened to them. Other screens made of 4' x 8' plywood, borrowed from the industrial arts shops, can be hinged or nailed in accordion folds supported by cleats nailed across the top. If the work cannot be nailed or pinned on the panels, strings or wires extended from nails and pins inserted in the top edge will suffice. A balanced saddle of wire suspended from the top can be improvised for heavy displays which are to be seen from the two sides of the screen.

To emphasize models or crafts, textured areas of pebbles and sand on the tables are effective. These areas should be shaped into simple free forms or geometric forms.

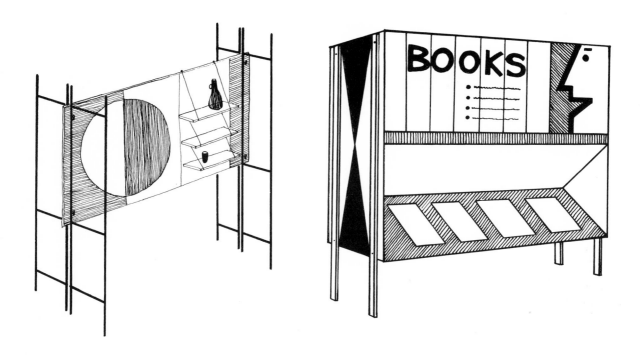

We should not err in the direction of stereotyped display design. Students are constantly
exposed to the most contemporary advertising,
and expect to find the same good taste and com-
pelling idiom in their schools. These examples
are ingenious constructions of simple materials, contemporary in spirit of design, and
thoroughly functional in purpose.

Corrugated cardboard, salvaged from boxes, is hinged with masking tape, covered with colored paper or painted with oil base paint to form an attractive space divider. Such table screens provide colorful backgrounds for the display of small items. Extending the idea to the larger exhibit, two sheets of plywood are temporarily fastened together. They serve to break space into intimate bays in which individual displays may be studied without the distraction of the complete exhibit.

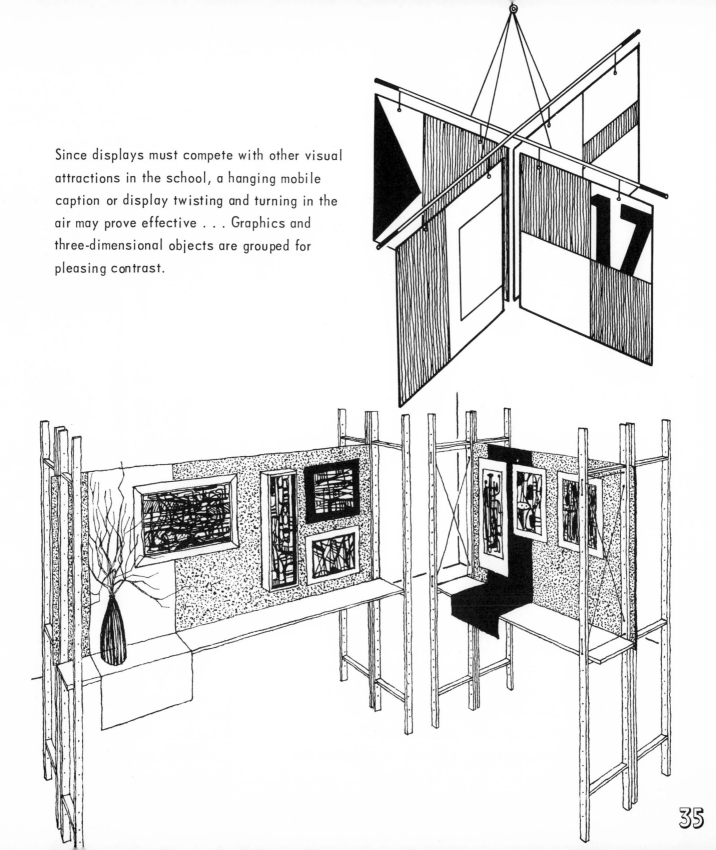

Since displays must compete with other visual attractions in the school, a hanging mobile caption or display twisting and turning in the air may prove effective . . . Graphics and three-dimensional objects are grouped for pleasing contrast.

More dynamic than the lateral display is the accordion-fold screen which articulates space and provides new viewing vistas as the spectator moves from area to area. Hinges, stovebolts, and wingnuts secure this portable screen.

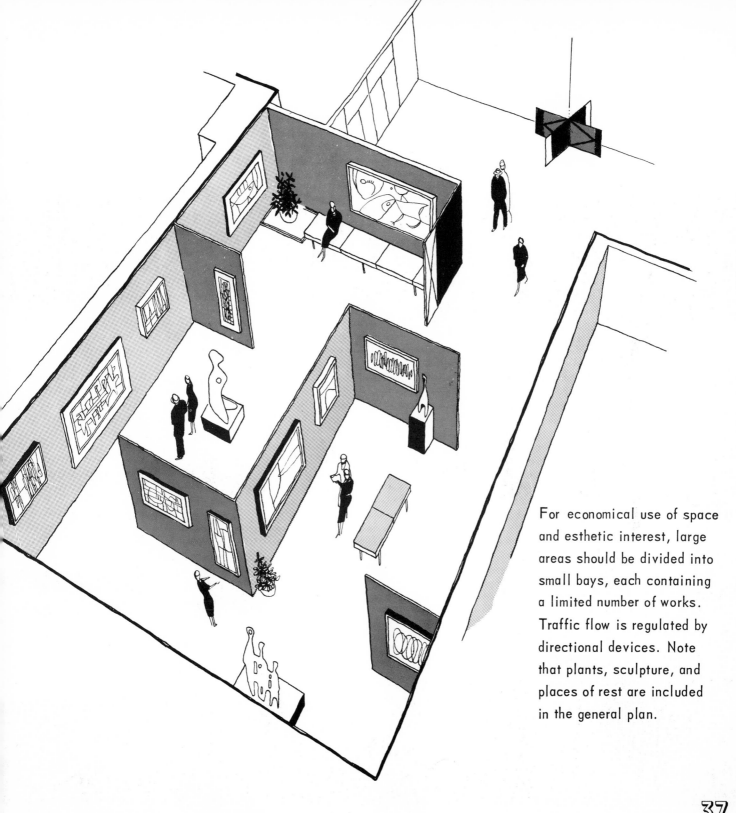

For economical use of space and esthetic interest, large areas should be divided into small bays, each containing a limited number of works. Traffic flow is regulated by directional devices. Note that plants, sculpture, and places of rest are included in the general plan.

37

HENRY GALLERY — UNIVERSITY OF WASHINGTON

◀ Notice how traffic can
move through this display.

OTHER ACCESSORIES

We should not overlook the shapes and bright colors of plants and flowers which make a colorful contribution to the arrangement. Painted wooden blocks cut from 2" x 4" or 4" x 4" stock elevate small objects to provide importance in height and a change in visual rhythm; larger three-dimensional objects, pottery, sculpture, or models are often placed on floor beds of textured material contained in frames made from strips of wood about 2" x 4" in size. Bricks and concrete blocks are useful stands. Other improvised stands for small displays are cylindrical oatmeal containers and small boxes wrapped in construction paper and fastened with tape.

MECHANICAL MOTION DEVICES   There are several simple mechanical devices such as turntables and other battery-operated devices which attract attention by movement and serve to alleviate the static quality of display. Any mechanical appliance which invites participation such as push buttons or levers insures interest. Peep holes into closed displays or pages to be turned involve the spectator physically.

LIGHTING   To bring a display to its full realization add a spotlight which illuminates dark walls and heightens the drama of a presentation.

DEMONSTRATIONS   Exhibits become alive with interest when demonstrators or experimenters participate with tools and materials. Placards should explain the various steps and processes.

GALLERY ATTENDANT   Attendants, who should be identified by name cards, answer questions, guide visitors, and protect exhibits. An otherwise impersonal exhibition takes on new significance when the public meets a few of the contributors.

CATALOGS OR PROGRAM   As an effective means of publicizing the activities of the school, the program is an important device.

PUBLICIZE YOUR EXHIBIT   By means of effective publicity: radio, television, mimeographed invitations, letters, posters and newspaper articles, the entire community can be drawn to the school.

PORTABLE EXHIBITS   In every city, friendly merchants welcome pre-arranged and securely fastened portable exhibits which can be used throughout the city to advertise special aspects of the school program.

THREE DIMENSIONAL DISPLAY

What part of one's education is derived from tactile sensation? The eye tells only the visual part of the story and we must supplement these impressions with touch sensation, relating size to weight and object to texture. No classroom is complete without ample opportunities to feel and to explore the myriad objects in our physical world. It is in this area that the alert teacher will plan to relate the abstract world of ideas to visual forms and the physical reality of objects.

OBJECTS TO FEEL AND TO ENJOY :

- Collections borrowed locally
- Shells, weeds, cones, pebbles, models
- Insects and objects which the children can collect, flowers, plants, sculpture

WHERE TO PLACE THINGS TO FEEL :

- on improvised shelves over radiators
- on window ledges
- on a touch table
- on a sand table
- in book cases

IMPROVISED CASES   A simple plywood box, covered with a hinged window sash and padlocked, will protect those few borrowed items which should not be handled without supervision.

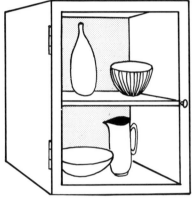
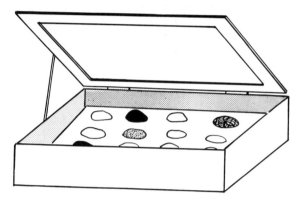

DISPLAY MATERIALS AS EFFECTIVE BACKGROUND   We have mentioned previously a number of materials which can provide backgrounds. Placed beneath the display the following surfaces will complement objects in color and texture:

- place mats
- sawdust
- sheets of cork
- pebbles

- linoleum
- colored paper
- corrugated paper
- sand

SIMPLE PRINCIPLES IN ARRANGING THREE DIMENSIONAL DISPLAYS

1. Keep the display simple, making several sequential arrangements in order to show all available material.

2. Vary the height of the objects shown by elevating some objects on bases.

3. Space is an element that can be manipulated by advancing some objects and by pushing others back so they appear to recede.

4. Balance several small objects on one side with a larger object; avoid formal balance.

5. Overlap some objects and create space between others for variety.

6. Observe color and texture contrast, mutually adjusting object to background. Consider the floor of the display case.

7. Provide captions which help explain the display.

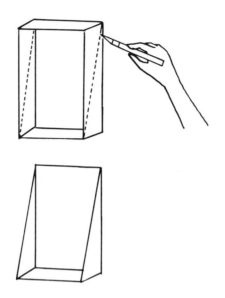

A cardboard box provides a shelf for object display and alleviates the flatness of the bulletin board. Interiors of the boxes may be painted or papered to introduce additional color . . . A string line effectively ties top and bottom areas into a harmonious whole . . . Strong in pattern and value contrast, the checkerboard variation carries well in the classroom. Light and dark areas become background for copy and illustration.

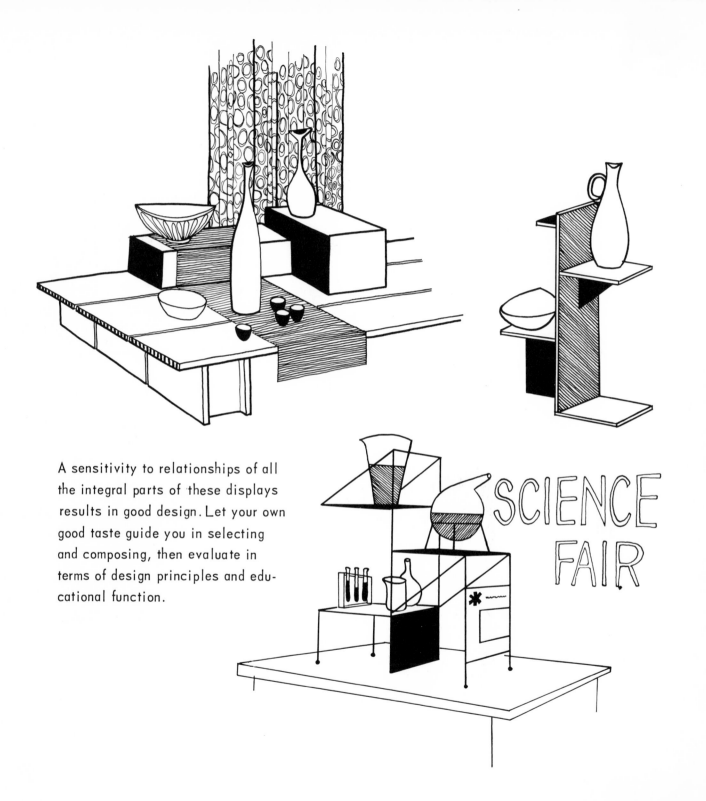

A sensitivity to relationships of all the integral parts of these displays results in good design. Let your own good taste guide you in selecting and composing, then evaluate in terms of design principles and educational function.

SCIENCE FAIR

In display cases the captions may be suspended by threads and organized in depth, some advancing toward the spectator and others falling back into space. Colors and paper textures chosen to complement the displayed items add to the beauty of the cases. Small folded cards stand beside their objects. Blocks of wood, dadoed with the saw, hold paper or cardboard labels. The cantilever block, below, is an effective one.

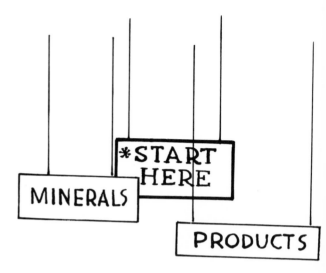

MINERALS

*START HERE

PRODUCTS

TOOLS

WHY VOTE

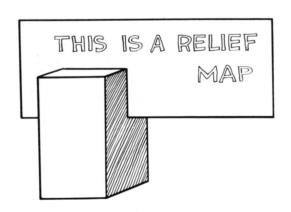

THIS IS A RELIEF MAP

A quality of spaciousness enhances each of the varied textures appearing in this composition of interlocking rectangles, page 45. ▶

TRIENNALE • FINLAND'S DISPLAY IN MILAN

LETTERING AND LABELING

The first requisite of all good display lettering, legibility at a planned distance, involves the selection of a suitable alphabet in the spirit of the display, good spacing and contrast of background and letters. Exciting the viewer, intellectually, and creating a desire to explore the display, visually, are the responsibility of the caption, which may take the form of a question — personal, direct, and concisely stated. Generally the caption contains only one idea. To give emphasis to those parts which are highly significant, size and contrasting backgrounds may be exaggerated. The labels or captions adjacent to the illustration and in line with the mounting edges, are placed on the eye level of the display and should be expressed in appropriate reading vocabulary. Individual labels, for the purpose of identification, provide the name, age, and grade of the exhibitor and, if the story portrayed can be abbreviated to form the title, adults are certain to find the display more meaningful. Lengthy explanatory copy is uninteresting and not read by most viewers. Important parts may be emphasized by the use of arrows, dots, darts, or lines — devices which help to create unity and provide accents.

The cut-paper letter is spaced directly on the background and secured with pins at the corners. To create a three-dimensional effect, letters may be pulled away from the background the length of the pins securing them to it. Commercial alphabets — cardboard, plaster pin-backs, gummed-back letters, and wooden letters may be used. Cut out letters from magazines and newspapers must be used with caution.

TYPE FORMS WHICH SHOW DIFFERENT STYLES

ABCDEFGHIJKLMNOPQRSTU
VWXYZ   1234567890

A simple, strong, block letter appropriate for copy or titles. Easy to cut or render in pen, the alphabet is appropriate for distance viewing if constructed in sufficient weight.

ABCDEFGHIJKLMNOPQRSTU
VWXYZ   SPEED ACTION

An alphabet with the connotation of action and movement is the slant letter. Any letter which has good proportion, thickness, and style lends itself to this variation. Uniformity of angle must be maintained for consistency.

ABCDEFGHIJKLMNOPQRSTUVWXYZ

Where it is necessary to conserve space, the condensed letter is appropriate but should never be used at the cost of legibility. Both condensed and extended letters should be practiced until one is able to fill a given space without apparent effort. Even color, a term used by advertising artists, refers to an even distribution of mass without dark spots. For example, two vertical letters occurring together appear to merge unless additional space is included between the letters.

47

iRREGULAR

The novelty alphabet of irregular letters is currently popular with advertising artists and may be useful in the classroom. Its connotation is quite different from the regular letter and must be clearly related to the mood of the display. Care in the design will prevent a highly decorative but illegible letter.

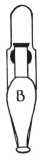

ABCDEFGHIJKLMN
OPQRSTUVWXYZ
abcdefghijklmnop
qrstuvwxyz,.?sag!

LETTERING WITH THE FLAT AND ROUND NIB POINT

The most important rule to remember in lettering the Gothic alphabet on page 47 and the script alphabet on this page is that the point must be held down evenly. Each point has a flat surface which must glide over the paper. Both upper and lower cases of the Gothic alphabet are based on a combination of the circle and straight line; for example, c, d, g, o, etc., are parts of the circle. As indicated by the example in the lower right hand corner, the script alphabet is easy to letter if a constant 45° angle is maintained. Never change this angle. The round letters appear slightly elliptic because they are composed of thick and thin strokes, but they, too, are based on the circle. Do not carry too much ink on the pen; dip more often. Constant practice will insure skill.

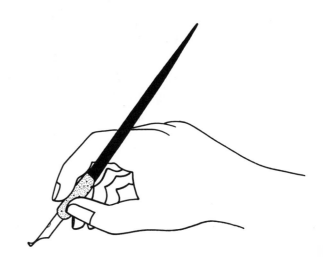

ABCDEFGHIJKLMNOP
QRSTUVWXYZ
1234567789

Exceptionally good for large lettering, the
steel brush can be mastered with practice.
The pen is held exactly like the ''C'' point
which is shown on page 49. Thick and thin
letters are produced without varying the 45°
angle at any time. Generally speaking the
letters in this alphabet can be spaced closely. To maintain the steel brush in good con-
dition the point should be washed in warm
water, without bending the steel bristles,
at the conclusion of the lettering exercise.

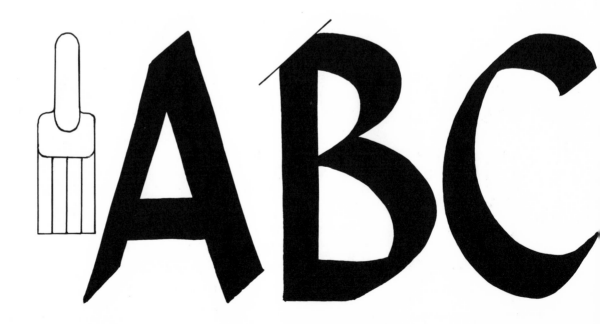

Letters are spaced optically, each receiving its individual needs according to its weight and character. There must be no merging of letters which create dark spots, nor on the other hand, should letters separate visually because of an abundance of space.

SPACING

Parallel strokes (IE, AV, etc.) must be given additional space between letters.

Circular letters occurring together (OO, PO, etc.) should be closely spaced.

Open letters (C, K, L, etc.) must be closely fitted with subsequent letters (CO, KO, etc.)

Horizontal strokes occurring in E, F, T, L, must be shortened to preserve even color in spacing.

Two useful tools are the "T" square and drawing board, when accurate letters or lining of charts is attempted.

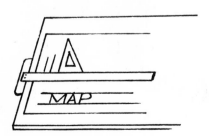

Hold the chalk around the center while applying even pressure to create straight block letters.

For this diagonal letter hold the chalk as shown, never changing the 45° position. Use for both the round and straight letter.

Chalk and crayon lettering is demonstrated in a variety of techniques: side and point, condensed and extended letters. Directional devices, similar to those at right, may be cut from construction paper; pins at the four corners are used to secure them to the background. Devices may be pulled out from the background to the length of the pins to create a feeling of depth.

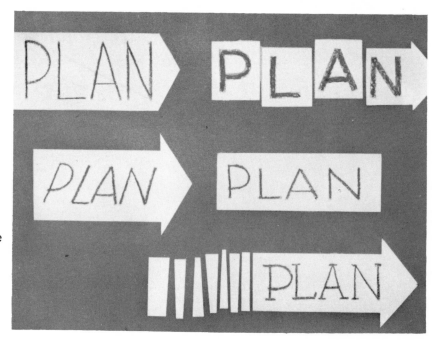

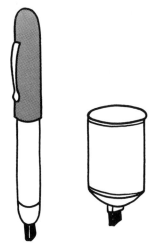

Stationery supply stores in every locality stock various types of pens and interesting gadgets for lettering. The most common is the felt-tip pen. Bottle pens with felt tips and inks in several colors have proved practical lettering tools for busy teachers.

One of the most useful alphabets is the cut-letter alphabet which can easily be reduced or enlarged. The proportion of the folded paper can vary from the square to the thin rectangle since all letters with the exception of the "i" are a consistent width. The letters "m" and "w" may be widened if desired. Using this model as a point of departure only, cut several alphabets of this type, varying the size from the four-inch letter to the two-inch, and place in an envelope in your display kit. See page 53.

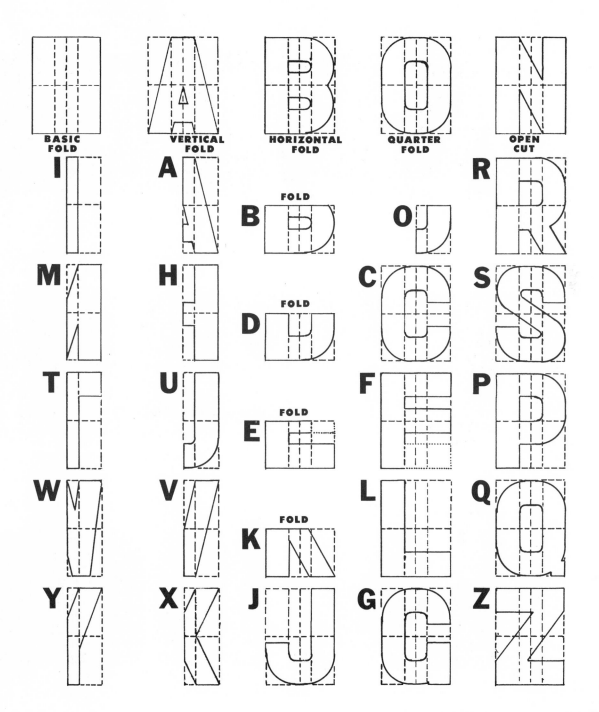

BASIC FOLD · VERTICAL FOLD · HORIZONTAL FOLD · QUARTER FOLD · OPEN CUT

53

ABCDE
FGHIJK
LMNOP

QRSTU

VWXYZ

SPACE

MATTING, MOUNTING AND HANGING

The mat, a cardboard or paper frame with a cutout window, and the paper mount on which the illustration is fastened with paste or pins, have a number of common purposes: to provide a means of emphasis, to separate the illustration from the background, and to complement in color. Mats and mounts provide a finished appearance and contribute harmony of repeated shape and color. From the colors found in the illustration itself comes the clue to the selection of a harmonizing mat, and this should be repeated without the distraction of additional new colors. News paper clippings and small pictures, often insignificant in size when standing alone, assume greater importance when they are grouped on a mount of construction paper.

Strips of masking tape are placed sticky side up beneath two corners.

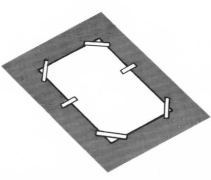

The mat is lowered into place and adjusted before coming into contact with the masking tape.

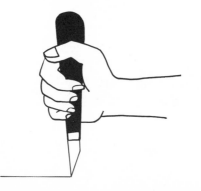

The mat and illustration are reversed and pressure applied to the corner tapes. Add additional strips of tape to the sides if necessary.

Mats and mounts are intended to enhance the illustration; pinched proportions will destroy the feeling of spaciousness a mat should provide. Generally a three-inch margin on top and sides, and a four-inch margin at the bottom are satisfactory proportions.

In the horizontal mat the same system of proportions is carried out with a generous bottom margin.

Multiple units may be matted together when they are harmonious in color and design. Avoid the "stairstep" or diagonal plan.

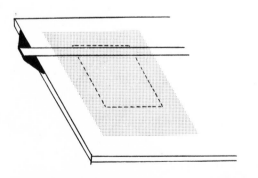 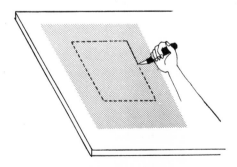

With the aid of T—square or straight edge draw all lines lightly. Thin mat boards should be measured, lined, and cut from the reverse side; thick mat boards must be handled face up in the event that the cut does not completely penetrate. Materials for matting and mounting are: bristle board, colored construction paper, pebble mat board, reverse side of wallpaper, and drawing paper. Cutting tools may be improvised from razor blades, preferably single edge, but a double edge may be taped for safety, mat knife, or sharp jackknife.

HANGING PICTURES AND PRINTS

If pictures are to be suspended from a picture molding, the wires should hang vertically in order to repeat the lines of the room; the ugly triangle of wires suspended from a single support should be avoided. Pictures should conceal wires, nails, or hooks if no moulding is available.

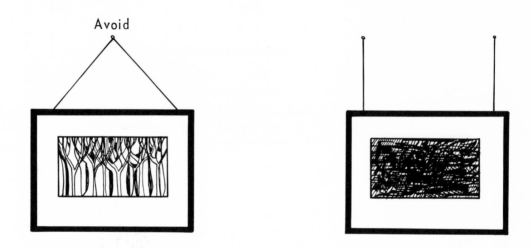

Avoid

An exhibit should express orderly arrangement of all units. Illustrations should be organized on a consistent top or bottom line. Small units must be grouped into series of three or four. Allow a rest space between groupings now and then.

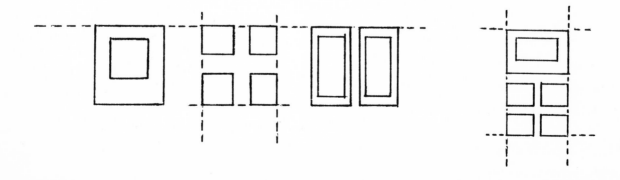

Our homes and classrooms should reflect our own good taste in the selection of pictures and prints and their sensitive placement on our walls. These should be selected on the basis of design, appealing subject, and color. Pictures should never be placed above eye-level of the observer.

Small pictures in series may be grouped horizontally or vertically but never diagonally.

Here a quantity of material is effectively grouped on the accordion-fold screen. Observe the handling of small illustrations and captions.

An opening caption of unusual beauty, simplicity, and restraint. Groupings of prints illustrate the principle of the rest space.

ART INSTITUTE OF CHICAGO, CHICAGO, ILLINOIS

10

BULLETIN BOARDS IN ACTION

The usefulness of this vital means of communication is limited only by the imagination which fails to see the rich visual possibilities of the subject and the exciting contribution of color, texture, and shapes in presenting an idea. Helping to create the kind of atmosphere which encourages learning is the purpose of an active bulletin board. Once the idea — a question, a picture, or newspaper clipping presents itself, it must be organized and expressed in material which will attract and hold attention.

In the next few pages, the page arrangements suggest simple basic layouts which can be varied to serve the many different kinds of classroom requirements. An uncluttered organization based on the horizontal and vertical line provides an easy eye pattern to important parts. Its endless variations make it one of the most useful of layouts. When ample negative space (open space) surrounds a limited number of illustrations, visual impact is assured.

1

1 Salvaged colored construction paper makes icicle shapes for this bulletin board.

2

2 Observe that the organization of straight lines is the basis for the layouts in this photo.

3 Wooden or cardboard boxes make excellent display shelves for three-dimensional material.

3

1

(Note the dotted lines which tie the illustrations on this page into one unit.)

1 Here, torn paper letters give the feeling of coral and sand. A large collection of shells was displayed on a nearby table.

2 Like a classroom map, a chart or graph may often be a direct teaching device.

3 The traditional symbols of any country attract attention and carry meaning.

4 A bulletin board with movable parts can be used for a complete unit of study.

2

3

4

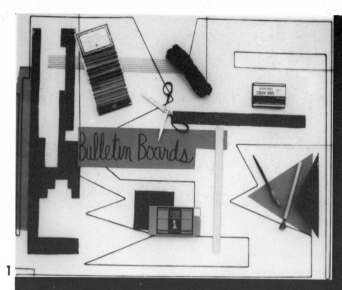

1 A variety of useful bulletin board materials provides answer to the question — what shall we use?

2 Cord, yarn, or string may be used if the captions are legible.

3 A few pictures and a caption tell the story; bulletin boards need not be elaborate.

4 Cut paper pinned in three-dimensional forms focuses attention on the important date. This idea is useful in any unit of study when illustrations are not available.

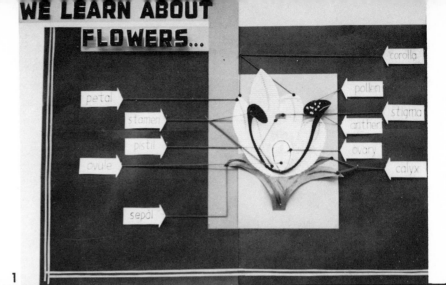

WE LEARN ABOUT FLOWERS...

corolla

petal

stamen

pollen

pistil

stigma

anther

ovule

ovary

calyx

sepal

1

WHAT TIME IS IT?

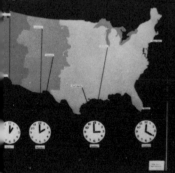

2

1 A similar idea can explain parts of the human body, a motor, an oil well, or mine.

2 Applying this idea to a map of the world, we might ask, "What Time is it in Bombay, Hong Kong, Tel Aviv?"

PIÑATA

3

4 **FRACTION FUN**

1 whole

1/2 1/2

1/4 1/4

1/4 1/4

3 Imagine other crafts which symbolize foreign countries.

4 Equally effective are scraps of wood or squares of paper cut into fractions. Materials are easily substituted.

1

2

3

4

1 A single "catchy" caption and a one-picture bulletin board is often sufficient to catch the eye.

2 After class discussion of Good Citzenship, the decisions written or lettered on blank strips of colored paper. Use idea of the "progressive bulletin board" in many other wo to illustrate the results of class discussion or current eve

3 A clever and simple illustration, applicable to many other topics, can be created by everyone.

4 Sure to appeal to children is this three-dimensional design cut paper. For other paper sculpture ideas consult the bib ography, page 72.

1

1 An excellent layout with a good idea for teaching. Note that the dots in both horizontal and vertical lines tie the design together. This idea is useful in the exposition type of bulletin board in which various steps are explained. For example, "How to Make a Kite," "How to Play a Game," "How the President Is Elected," are appropriate topics.

2 Every school has a quantity of notices which must be organized effectively. Here blocks of paper and lines connect the irregular checkerboard. Wherever possible edges are uniform and ample negative space is allowed.

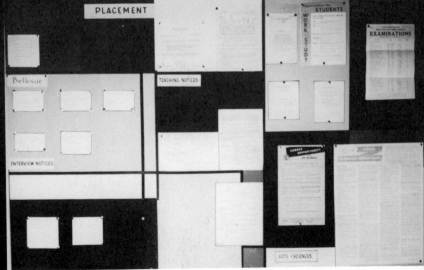

2

1

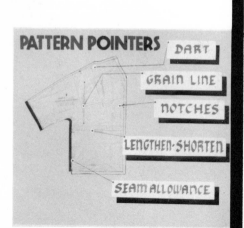

2

3

1 Watch department store windows, current magazines and papers for good holiday ideas. Bulletin boards should express a contemporary attitude if they are to attract attention.

2 In this progressive-type bulletin board, the lists of words may be changed as errors in pronunciation are heard in class. The same idea may be used in learning a foreign language.

3 When possible, show an actual object to illustrate the point.

4 Relating the term to a graphic explanation simplifies new vocabulary. This idea applies to science, learning to read a map, or industrial arts training.

4

The layout of this page suggests an effective use of illustrations only. When time is short, captions may be omitted entirely. Bulletin boards should not consume a great deal of time in preparation; "instant" displays consisting of one picture or clipping with an organization of lines or arrows are effective.

COURTESY OF WASHINGTON STATE ART GUIDE

 Seeing, thinking, comparing, experimenting will improve your use of this effective means of communication. Avoid the traditional and the trite. What you do with bulletin boards and display in your classes is up to you!

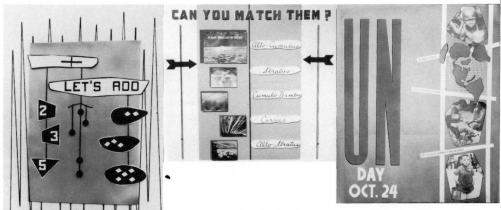

CHART FOR TEACHERS

AGE GROUP	SOCIAL INTERESTS	DEVELOPMENTAL LEVEL	SUBJECT INTERESTS	SPECIFIC REQUIREMEN
Primary Level K-1—2—3	Parallel play in early stages. Interest in small groups. Developing group activity, emerging leadership and followship. Developing sense of group responsibility.	Active, curious. Vocabulary developing rapidly with experience. Interest in "what", "why", and "how". What makes things work? Satisfied with reasonable answers. Enjoy humor. Tactile experience important. Big muscle control.	Pets, animals, insects, natural phenomena (rain, snow, ice). Machines, motion. Immediate family. Boats, trains, etc.	Large size type for labels, primer-size type and pre-primer type, manuscript lettering, large, simple layouts on vision level, three-dimensional objects to handle. Can collect and select but cannot arrange displays In 3rd grade can help arrange displays. Keeps displays in order.
Intermediate Level 4—5—6	Expanding interests into world. Group participation and cooperation. Likes challenge.	Muscular control. Expresses himself. Close ties with family. Active. Broad interests and inquisitive.	Motors, sports, Animals. Camping, outdoor life. Science. Health. Wide interest in art.	Color, intrigue interest through moving parts; captions in form of questions. How things work. Child able to arrange display with guidance, cut letters. Committee work is effective
Junior High School 7—8—9	Interest in success. Intense friendships. Interest in opposite sex. Desire to assert personality, often rebellious, critical, often religious, likes adventure.	Develops ability to manipulate small parts. Developing adult bodies. Sex interests. Capable of planning display and installing it.	Mechanics, sports, music, jazz. Etiquette, how to do something. Dating, dress, grooming, hobbies.	Catchy phrases or contemporary language, bright col strong in contrast, fast mov ing and hold attention.
Senior High School	Interest in opposite sex. Marriage, families, vocations, new interest and appreciation of family developing. Preparing to take place in world.	Adult abilities. Can plan and execute displays.	Same, material on families, vocations, college, hobbies, politics, etc.	Educational display. Diagrams, charts. Reading charts. Reading for information. All adult interests.

70

SOURCES FOR SUPPLIES

FROM YOUR HARDWARE STORE . . . .

Brushes, Paint
Glue
Nails
Rope
Sandpaper
Staplers

String
Tacks
Small Tools
Varnish
Wire
Wire Screening

WHERE TO GET SUPPLIES

The most important thing is to be resourceful; improvised materials may give you the desired effect. Listed here are some sources for staple items you may need to buy.

FROM YOUR SCHOOL SUPPLIES DEALER OR VARIETY STORE . . . .

Aluminum Foil
Brushes, Artists'
Buttons
Cellophane
Chalk
Corrugated Cardboard
Crayons
Inks, black and colored
Paints,
    tempera and water color
Paper, colored construction

Paste
Pens, felt nib
Pens, lettering
Pins with colored heads
Pipe Cleaners
Ribbon
Rubber Cement
Scissors
Tape
Yarn

ALPHABETS AND LETTERS

Dick Blick, Galesburg, Illinois

Arthur Brown and Brothers, Inc., 2 West 46th St., New York, N.Y. 10036

Mitten's Display Letters, 345 Fifth Street, Redlands, California

Mutual Aids, 1946 Hillhurst, Los Angeles, California 90047

SOME REGIONAL SCHOOL SUPPLIES DISTRIBUTORS

J. L. Hammett Co.
    Kendall Square, Cambridge, Mass.
    2393 Vauxhall Road, Union, New Jersey
    165 Water St., Lyons, New York

Garrett-Buchanan Company
    10th & Spring Garden Sts., Philadelphia, Pa. 19123

The Dobson-Evans Co.
    1100 W. 3rd Ave., Columbus, Ohio 43212

J. R. Holcomb Co.
    1710 E. 22nd St., Cleveland, Ohio 44114

Michigan School Service Inc.
    Lansing, Michigan 48902

James & Law Co.
    217 W. Main St., Clarksburg, West Va. 26301

Virginia School Equipment Co., Inc.
    104 S. Foushee St., Richmond, Va. 23220

Beckley-Cardy Co.
    1900 N. Narragansett, Chicago, Illinois 60639

Modern School Supply
    3810 E. 16th S., Indianapolis, Indiana 46207

Minneapolis School Supply Co.
    173 N. W. Bank Bldg., Minneapolis, Minn. 55402

Hoover Brothers, Inc.
    1511 Baltimore, Kansas City, Missouri 64108

H. R. Meininger Co.
    409 Sixteenth St., Denver, Colorado 80202

J. K. Gill & Co.
    408 Fifth Ave., S. W., Portland, Oregon 97204

Northern School Supply Co.
    P. O. Box 431, Great Falls, Montana 59401

Educators Furniture & Supply Co., Inc.
    5912 R. Street, Sacramento, California 95817

Practical Drawing Co.
    P. O. Box 5388, Dallas, Texas 75222

Standard School Service, Inc.
    1945 Hoover Ct., Birmingham, Alabama 35226

Moyer-Vico Ltd.
    25 Milvan Drive, Weston, Ontario, Canada

BIBLIOGRAPHY

Audio-Visual Instruction: Materials and Methods, James W. Brown, Richard B. Lewis and
Fred F. Harcleroad, McGraw-Hill, New York, 1964

Audio-Visual Materials and Techniques, Second Edition, James S. Kinder, American Book Co
New York, 1959

Audio-Visual Materials, Walter Wittich & Charles Schuller, Harper & Brothers, 1962

A Basic Guide to Lettering, Robert D. Buckley, Greenberg, New York, 1951

Bulletin Boards for Teaching, Charles H. Dent and Ernest F. Tiemann, Visual Instruction
Bureau, Division of Extension, University of Texas, Austin, Texas, 1955

Creating With Paper, Pauline Johnson, University of Washington Press, Seattle, 1959

Display for Learning, East & Dale, Dryden Press, New York, N. Y.

Education Exhibits: How to Prepare and Use Them, A Manual for Extension Workers, H. W.
Gilbertson, U. S. Department of Agriculture, Miscellaneous Publication
No. 634, Washington, D. C., January 1948

Educational Displays and Exhibits, J. Preston Lockridge, Visual Instruction Bureau, Division of Extension, University of Texas, Austin, Texas, 1959

Exhibitions, Klaus Frank, Frederick Praeger, New York, N. Y. 1961

Instructional Materials, Louis Shores, Ronald Press Co., New York, 1960

Planning and Producing Audio Visual Materials, Jerrold E. Kemp, Chandler Publishing Co.,
San Francisco

Preparing Visual Instructional Materials, Ed Minor, McGraw-Hill Book Co., New York, 1962

Space, Arrangement, Beauty in School, Association for Childhood Education International,
Washington, D. C., 1958 – 1959

MOTION PICTURES

Better Bulletin Boards; Sound, Black and White, 10 minutes, Indiana University

Bulletin Boards, An Effective Teaching Device; Revised in 1966, Sound, Color, 11 minutes,
Reino Randall, Bailey Films, Inc., 6509 De Longpre Ave., Hollywood, California 90028

FILM STRIPS

Bulletin Boards, Many Examples of a Variety of Bulletin Boards, 40 frames, Silent, Color,
Bailey Films, Inc., Reino Randall, 6509 De Longpre Ave., Hollywood, California 90028

How to Keep Your Bulletin Boards Alive, 32 frames, Silent, Color, Teaching Aids Laborator
Ohio State University

Museum Techniques, 37 frames, Silent, Black and White, Herbert E. Budek Co.

DAVIS PRESS, INC., WORCES